ISBN 960-7254-45-7

© 1997 KAPON EDITIONS

Makriyanni 23-27, 117 42 Athens
Tel./fax: (01) 92 14089, 7241442

JULIA VOKOTOPOULOU
Director of the Archaeological Museum of Thessalonike

G SHORT GUIDE

TO THE ARCHAEOLOGICAL MUSEUM OF THESSALONIKE

KAPON EDITIONS

CONTENTS

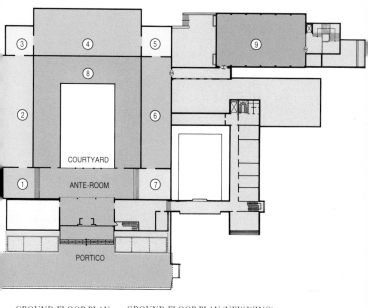

COURTYARD

ANTE-ROOM

PORTICO

GROUND-FLOOR PLAN   GROUND-FLOOR PLAN (NEW WING)

INTRODUCTION

The Archaeological Museum of Thessalonike, the work of the architect Patroklos Karantinos, was inaugurated on 27 October 1962, and the display in all the galleries was completed in 1971. It includes sculptures, the prehistoric collection, miniature works of art from the Archaic and Classical periods, and the brilliant group of finds from the tombs at Derveni, which was first presented to the public in 1962 on the day of the inauguration.

A few years later, in 1978, the dazzling finds from Vergina necessitated the first change to the display: objects from the royal tombs were exhibited in the area occupied by the prehistoric collection and miniature art, as part of the exhibition 'Treasures of Ancient Macedonia'. The Vergina treasures and other valuable finds from the 1970s made it necessary to extend the museum building: the New Wing was inaugurated in July 1980 with the exhibition 'Alexander the Great'. The excavation of the cemetery at Sindos, so rich in gold, began in this same year and the exhibition of objects from Sindos was presented to the public in October 1982.

There followed the re-exhibition of the finds from Vergina and Derveni in 1984 and an exhibition on ancient Thessalonike in 1985, and in 1989 the new finds from ancient and Classical times were displayed in the ground floor of the New Wing.

No other museum in Greece has experienced the rapid increase in objects for display faced by the Archaeological Museum of Thessalonike in the last twenty years; the result has been frequent changes and additions to the original display of 1971, and the partial violation of the arrangement by successive periods on which the exhibition was organized. All that survives of the original display of 1971 is the sculpture exhibition which has been slightly modified.

Visitors to the museum may visit individual exhibitions (Vergina, Thessalonike, Sindos), depending on the amount of time at their disposal. If they wish to form a picture of the chronological evolution of culture in the area of Central Macedonia, they should begin their visit on the ground floor of the New Wing, where objects of prehistoric, Archaic and Classical times are on display (rooms 10-11), continue with objects from the 4th c. BC in the Vergina and Derveni room (room 9), and for the Hellenistic and Roman periods visit the Thessalonike room (room 4) and the sculpture exhibition (room 1-3, 5-6), which ends in the area of the Macedonian tombs (room 7). The sculptures surround the Sindos room (room 8), the exhibits in which date from the 6th and 5th c. BC.

1. Sarcophagus with a scene of battle and men disembarking from a ship on the front. 2nd-3rd c. AD (Portico).

SCULPTURE EXHIBITION

ANTE-ROOM

The grave stele of Agenor, a work of the 5th c. BC, from Ierissos in Chalkidiki (ancient Akanthos), is on temporary display here.

2-3. Part of a marble water-spout and a marble cornice from an Ionic temple in Thessalonike. Late 6th c. BC.

ROOM 1

Room 1 contains architectural members from an Archaic Ionic temple whose site has not been identified. This temple is associated with ancient Therme, a city that stood at the head of the Thermaic Gulf before the foundation of Thessalonike. Column capitals, drums and bases, cornices and thresholds, with richly

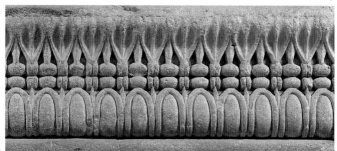

3

carved Lesbian and Ionic mouldings, and also a lion's head water spout, were found scattered in various parts of west Thessalonike. They date from the late 6th c. BC.

4. *Relief head of a youth maybe from the sculptural decoration of an Ionic temple in Thessalonike. Late 6th c. BC.*

5-6. *Archaic statues of a kouros and a kore from East Thrace. Late 6th c. BC.*

Room 2 is the first room of the sculpture display, which is organized in chronological sequence. The torsoes of a kouros and a kore from Redestos in East Thrace date from the late 6th c. BC. The piece of a grave stone with a relief figure of a kore, around 440 BC, is a work of some importance for our knowledge of local sculpture, while the masterful stele with the young girl holding a dove, from Nea Kallikrateia, another grave monument contemporary with the previous one, was made by a sculptor from Paros. Two original works from Olynthos, a terracotta protome of a goddess and a marble head of

youth or god, date from the late 5th c. BC. A number of Roman copies of 5th c. BC sculptures have been discovered in Thessalonike, amongst them parts of an acrolithic statue of Athena in a Pheidian type, from the early 3rd c. AD, the facial features of which are those of the empress Julia Domna, and the copy of a statue of Aphrodite, which is probably a replica of the Aphrodite 'of the Gardens' by Alkamenes, found in the Sarapeion in Thessalonike.

The grave stele from Potidaia with a relief figure of a youth holding a lyre, and a unique votive relief, dedicated to Hephais-

7. Marble head of a youth or god from Olynthos. 5th c. BC.

8. Stele of a young girl from Nea Kallikrateia. 5th c. BC.

9. *Statue of Aphrodite,*
in the so-called 'Frejus'
type. From the Sarapeion
in Thessalonike.

10. *Statue of a peplophoros.*
From the Sarapeion in
Thessalonike. 2nd c. AD.

11

ΛΥΣΘΕΝΗΣΗ ΡΑΙΣΤΙΩΝ ΗΡΩΙ

20

tion, the friend of Alexander the Great, are both 4th BC works. The group of Demeter and Kore, the statue of a priestess, and a marble inscribed altar from the sanctuary of Demeter in the area of ancient Lete (Derveni, Thessalonike), all date from the Hellenistic period.

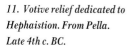

11. Votive relief dedicated to Hephaistion. From Pella. Late 4th c. BC.

12. Statue in the type of the 'Petite Herculanaise'. Hellenistic period.

12

13

ROOM 3

Room 3 contains Hellenistic sculptures dating mainly from the 2nd and 1st c. BC. Outstanding amongst them are a headless statue of a man wearing a himation, a realistic male head from a grave relief of the 1st c. BC, a larger-than-life-size head, possibly of Poseidon, and impressively large grave reliefs from Beroia and Lete; the latter bears the signature of the sculptor Euandros from Beroia (first half of the 1st c. BC). The bronze medallion from the decoration of a wooden chariot, with the masterful relief bust of Athena, is a recent find from Plateia Diikitiriou.

14

13. Bronze attachment for a wooden chariot with a bust of Athena. From Thessalonike. Hellenistic period.

14. Portrait from a grave relief. From Thessalonike. 1st c. BC.

15. *Two relief slabs from an imposing funerary monument from Lete. 2nd-1st c. BC.*

16. *Inscribed statue base from Thessalonike. From the ancient Agora. 2nd c. AD.*

15

THESSALONIKE EXHIBITION

ROOM 4

On the occasion of the 2,300th anniversary of the foundation of Thessalonike, which was celebrated with much festivity in 1985, an exhibition was organized on the history of Thessalonike from the prehistoric period to Christian times. The exhibition was mounted in room 4 and contained, in addition to new objects, the sculptures and mosaics from the city of Thessalonike which were already on display there.

Thessalonike was founded in 315 BC by King Cassander, who named it after his wife, the daughter of Philip II and sister of Alexander the Great. The foundation involved the com-

16

pulsory merger of the populations of 26 townships on the Thermaic Gulf, including Therme, the most important city before the foundation of Thessalonike. Two of these townships, the tumuli at Karambournaki and Toumba, which are the most likely candidates for identification with Therme, are the subject of the first section (A) of the exhibition (cases 1-7), together with a third site, the 'Gona' tumulus, near the airport. Imported Mycenaean and Geometric pottery is evidence for the direct contacts between the coastal settlements of the Thermaic Gulf and southern Greece, which continued and intensified in Archaic and Classical periods. Local jewellery made of precious metals is quite com-

17

mon in tombs, and is found together with choice clay pottery from Ionia, Corinth and Attica, and glass perfume vases from Phoenicia, and local pottery is present in great quantities in every period.

Cassander's Thessalonike, the city produced by the compulsory unification of the rich townships, is presented in the second unit (B: cases 10-15). For the early centuries of the life of the new city, which coincide with the Hellenistic period, our information is derived mainly from tombs. Six 'Macedonian' tombs have so far been found to

18

17-18. Terracotta female figurines from a tomb in Thessalonike. Late 3rd-2nd c. BC (case 13).

east and west of Thessalonike, all of which had been looted and contained only a few clay vases (cases 11-12). The simple pit graves in Melenikou Street have yielded a series of charming female figurines of the 3rd-2nd c. BC (case 13), while the grave of the young girl discovered at Neapolis (case 15) contains some fine gold jewellery, masterful figurines, and two precious vases made of glass and faience, imported from Egypt in the early 2nd c. BC.

The remaining and largest part of the exhibition (sections C-G) is devoted to Thessalonike in the Roman period, when the city was at its most flourishing and had attained the status of 'Mother of all Macedonia'. The wealth of the city is attested by finds from its extensive cemeteries (section C) – outstanding amongst them are the glass vases and birds (case 17) – and also by the large number of marble statues. Of particular interest is the group of statues of deities and priestesses, and also of votive reliefs from the Sarapeion (section D), that is, the sanctuary of the Egyptian gods – Sarapis, Isis, Osiris and Harpokrates – which was founded in the 3rd c. BC and functioned until at least the end of the 2nd c. AD. The heads from larger-than-life-size statues of Sarapis and Isis are highly impressive.

19-20. Terracotta female figurines from a tomb in Thessalonike. Late 3rd-2nd c. BC (case 13).

The opposite side of the room is devoted to the public buildings of Thessalonike (the palace of Galerius and the Agora, section F), and examples of the currency minted by the city are presented in case 21. The large mosaic floor with a scene of the meeting of Dionysos and Ariadne on Naxos gives some idea of the luxury of the buildings of Roman Thessalonike.

21-22. Terracotta naked puppet and female figurines from tombs in Thessalonike. 3rd-2nd c. BC (cases 13-14).

21

30

23. *Amulets of gold and semi-precious stones, from a tomb in Thessalonike.*
Hellenistic period (case 16).

24. *Faience basket from a tomb in Thessalonike. 200-150 BC (case 15).*

24

25

26

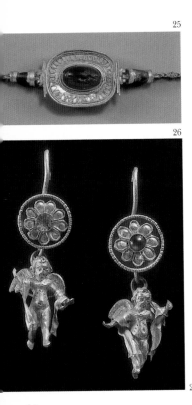

27

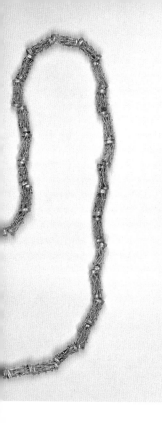

25-27. *Gold jewellery from the tomb of a girl at Neapolis near Thessalonike. 200-150 BC (case 15).*

28. *Gold jewellery from a cemetery dating from Roman times. 1st-3rd c. AD (case 18).*

28

29. *Glass perfume vases in the shape of a bird from tombs in Thessalonike. 1st c. AI*

30. Vases from tombs in Thessalonike. 1st-4th c. AD (case 17).

31-32. Terracotta groups of Eros and Psyche. From tombs in Thessalonike. Roman times (case 18).

33. Terracotta figurines depicting stock characters from ancient comedy. From a tomb in Thessalonike. 1st c. AD (case 20).

31

32

34. Detail of a grave stele with an enthroned female figure.
From a tomb in Thessalonike. Late Hellenistic period.

35. *Detail of a grave stele dedicated to Lucius Cornelius Neon.*
From a tomb in Thessalonike. 1st c. AD.

36

37

36. *Grave stele with a scene of a funeral banquet, dedicated to his wife Auge by Publius Maximus. From a tomb in Thessalonike. 1st c. BC.*

37. *Funeral altar dedicated to Marcus Varenius Areskon. Second half of the 2nd c. AD.*

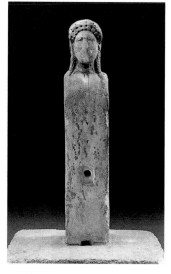

38. *Statue of Harpokrates, son of Sarapis and Isis.*
From the Sarapeion in Thessalonike. 2nd c. AD.

39. *Small marble herm from the Sarapeion in Thessalonike.*

40. *Detail of a votive stele dedicated to Osiris.*
From the Sarapeion in Thessalonike. Late 2nd c. BC.

40

41. *Statue of a priestess of Isis. From the Sarapeion in Thessalonike. Roman times.*

42. *Female statuette from Thessalonike. Roman times.*

43

50

43. *Marble head, probably from a statue of Isis. From the area of the Sarapeion. 1st c. AD.*

44. *Marble head of a statue of Sarapis. Roman copy of a 4th c. BC work.*

44

45. *Relief depicting the Celtic goddess Epona, sitting on a throne amongst four horses as goddess of the earth. Late Roman times.*

46. *Inscription on marble containing the text of a royal rescript of Philip V. From the Sarapeion. 186 BC.*

47. *Marble altar dedicated to Fulvius, deified son of the emperor Marcus Aurelius. AD 219.*

45

46

47

55

48. Part of a mosaic floor from a
Roman bath. A multi-coloured
guilloche frames two square panels in
which are set busts of Dionysos
(right) and a woman (left). 3rd c. AD.

49. Marble arch from the complex of Galerius, on which carved are frontal busts of the Caesar Galerius and the personified 'Fortune' of Thessalonike. 4th c. AD.

49

50

*50-51. Marble capitals from the Octagon in the complex of Galerius.
Late 3rd or early 4th c. AD.*

51

52

53

52-53. *Heads of marble statues. From the Roman Agora in Thessalonike. Roman times.*

54. *Statue of a Satyr from a fountain in Thessalonike. Roman times.*

54

55. *Part of a mosaic floor depicting a four-horse chariot. From a house in Thessalonike. 3rd c. AD.*

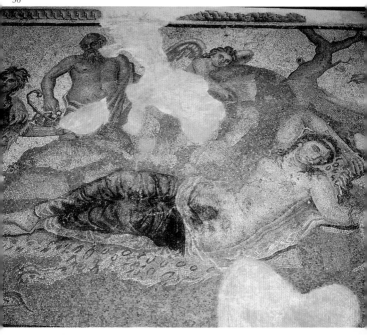

56. Detail from a mosaic floor from a house in Thessalonike depicting Ariadne on Naxos. Early 3rd c. AD.

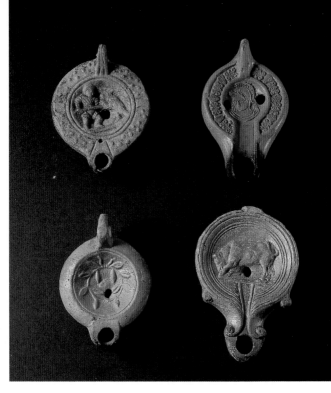

57. Terracotta lamps of Roman times. From Thessalonike (case 23).

58. Fragment of a red plate with relief decoration. 3rd c. AD (case 22).

SCULPTURE EXHIBITION

ROOM 5

The centre of the room is dominated by the statue of Octavius Augustus, which was probably made in Thessalonike during the time of the emperor Tiberius and is a copy of a bronze original, like the similar type of Augustus found at Prima Porta near Rome. The original was probably made about 19 BC when Augustus visited the East. It is one of the examples of the

59. *Funerary monument of Antigonos Eulandros. From Lete. About 30 BC.*

60. *Statue of the emperor Octavius Augustus. First half of the 1st c. AD.*

61. *Headless statue of the emperor Claudius. About AD 50.*

60

61

62

series of statues that Rome erected for propaganda purposes in various nerve-centres of the empire. It is surrounded by realistic portraits of the 1st c. AD, some of which belong to circular grave reliefs (a type known as *imago clipeata*).

The headless statue of the emperor Claudius (about AD 50) belongs to the same category as the statue of Augustus. Two other notable items are the head of a goddess dating from the Hellenistic period, which was converted in the 1st c. AD into a portrait, a common practice in Roman times, and another monumental grave relief from Lete, the monument of Antigonos Eulandros (about 30 BC).

62. Circular grave relief
(imago clipeata). Middle of the 1st c. AD.

63. Marble head of a goddess of Hellenistic
date, which was converted into a portrait in the
second quarter of the 1st c. AD.

ROOM 6

The torso of a statue of the emperor Hadrian at the entrance to this room is surrounded by a display of sculpture from his time (2nd c. AD). One notable example is the portrait of a young girl with sensitively modelled flesh. On the wall are pieces of a gold-embroidered cloth from a 4th c. AD burial.

The rest of the room contains realistic or idealized portraits,

64. Torso of a statue of the emperor Hadrian. 2nd c. AD.

65. Piece of a gold-embroidered cloth from a 4th c. AD burial.

66. Portrait of a young girl. 2nd c. AD.

64

65

66

67

67. *Portrait of a male figure from the second half of the 2nd c. AD.*

68. *Herm with the bust of a bearded youth. Second half of the 2nd c. AD.*

frequently in the type of the philosopher, grave reliefs of popular art, a funeral banquet and parts of sarcophagi, which are representative of the various cultural and artistic currents of Late Antiquity. Outstanding amongst these are the marble portrait of Septimius Severus (AD 193-211), the bronze head of Alexander Severus (AD 222-235) from Ryakia in Pieria, a larger-than-life-size statue in the type of the 'Petite Herculanaise', of the same period, and portraits of men and women dating from the 4th and 5th c. AD.

Realistic sculpture has clearly given way to the expressive power of lines and outlines, which better represented the austere spiritual world of the Christian era.

69

70

69. *Female statue in the type of the 'Petite Herculanaise'. About AD 200.*

70. *Popular grave relief. 4th c. AD.*

72

71

71. *Portrait of the emperor Septimius Severus. Late 2nd c. AD.*

72. *Bronze head of Alexander Severus. From Pieria. First half of the 3rd c. AD.*

73-74. *Busts of a couple from Thessalonike. Late Antiquity (4th c. AD).*

*75. Part of an Attic sarcophagus, depicting the hunt for the Calydonian boar.
Early 3rd c. AD.*

THE MACEDONIAN TOMBS

About the middle of the 4th c. BC rich Macedonians and their kings buried their dead in majestic subterranean monuments, known to archaeology as Macedonian tombs, since the architectural type was created in Macedonia. They are stone buildings with one or two chambers and roofed with a vault. Their façades reproduce the architectural features of temples, are surmounted by a pediment, and are most often painted, as also is the interior. After the interment, the subterranean tomb was covered by enormous quantities of earth, which formed a conical tumulus.

The Macedonian tombs were family monuments. The dead were placed on wooden or marble couches. If they had been cremated, the cinerary urn was placed on a bench, amongst other rich offerings, usually precious vases and personal objects. Because of the value of their content, the Macedonian tombs are rarely found undisturbed, like the two royal tombs at Vergina.

The tombs at Ayia Paraskevi in Thessalonike and at Potidaia are no exception to the rule. The very few terracotta figurines (wall case) left behind by the grave-robbers, date from the late 4th c. BC. In front of the life-size painted reconstruction of the façade of the tomb at Ayia Paraskevi is exhibited the mar-

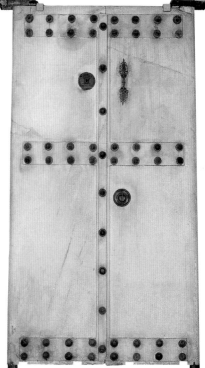

*76. The marble door
from the Macedonian
tomb at Ayia Paraskevi
in Thessalonike.
Late 4th c. BC.*

ble double door, 2.4 m. high, which led from the antechamber to the main chamber of the tomb. The door is unique both for its technical perfection and for the excellent state of preservation of the decorative bronze attachments.

From the tomb at Potidaia are displayed the plain stone door and two marble couches with painted decoration. The subject on the upper cross-piece is an open-air shrine: reclining gods and goddesses, Aphrodite, and Dionysos, and a Silenus relax in the sacred grove, in which can be seen a spring, a statue, the young Herakles, and a deer eating the tender leaves of a tree. This is a monument of considerable importance for our knowledge of ancient Greek painting.

77

*77. The marble couches from the
Macedonian tomb at Potidaia.
Late 4th c. BC.*

*78. Detail from the painted
decoration of the couches of the
tomb at Potidaia.*

SINDOS EXHIBITION

Near modern Sindos, near Thessalonike, there is an ancient settlement, probably ancient Chalastra, which is surrounded by cemeteries. In 1980-1982, 121 tombs were excavated covering a single period in the long life of the city, from the middle of the 6th to the middle of the 5th c. BC. Though these were simply constructed pit or cist graves of poros, they contained large numbers of often valuable offerings (objects placed in tombs), which provide very important infor-

79. Attic black-figure lekythos. Sindos, tomb 65. 550-540 BC (case 8).

80. Inscribed gold finger-ring. Sindos, tomb 111. About 430 BC (case 9).

81. Attic red-figure krater. Sindos, tomb 55. 460-450 BC (case 3).

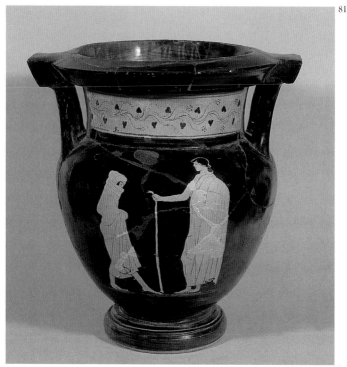

82. *Amber necklace. Sindos, tomb 20. 510-500 BC (case 13).*

83. *Biconical pendant made of gold sheet. Sindos, tomb 20. 510-500 BC (case 15).*

84. *Silver pins with elaborate gold heads. Sindos, tomb 20. 510-500 BC (case 13).*

83

84

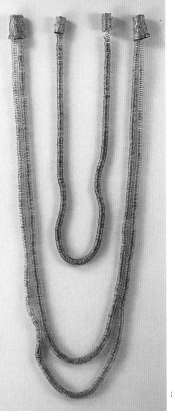

mation concerning trade, the arts, and society in a small Macedonian city in the Archaic and Early Classical periods.

A striking feature of the graves was the discovery of large quantities of gold jewellery, and also of items made of gold sheet destined for funeral use, such as the lozenge-shaped mouthpieces used to seal the mouth of the dead, the five gold masks, and the vast number of gold strips that adorned their garments. Quite apart from the custom that gave rise to this usage, it would not have been possible if there had not been an abundance of the raw material, gold,

85-86. Superb gold and silver necklaces. Sindos, tomb 20. 510-500 BC (case 16).

in the sand of the neighbouring river Gallikos, the ancient name of which was Echeidoros ('gift-bearing'). Thanks to these two circumstances, the tombs of Sindos have revealed the high level attained by gold-working and metallurgy in general in Ancient Macedonia, and have shown that the 4th century acme was not due to influences from workshops in southern Greece, but was the result of a long local tradition in the arts. In the 6th c. BC, the goldsmiths of Chalastra were masters of two very difficult techniques: filigree and granulation.

The vases and terracotta figurines found at Sindos indicate that there was a lively trade with Ionia, Attica and Corinth. Another category of grave offer-

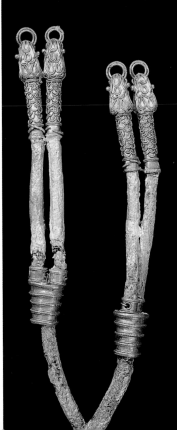

87. *Iron model of a waggon pulled by terracotta figurines of mules. Sindos, tomb 59. 530-520 BC (case 17).*

88. *Bronze 'Illyrian' helmets with applied gold strips. Sindos, tombs 25 and 59. 540-530/20 BC (cases 20 and 21).*

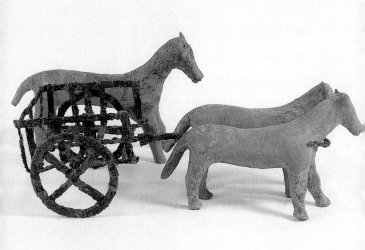

91

89. *Miniature Attic kylikes.*
Sindos, tomb 25. About 540 BC
(case 25).

90. *Plastically modelled vase in*
the form of a cock, from an Ionian
workshop. Sindos, tomb 25.
About 540 BC (case 25).

90

91. Gold sheet that adorned the breast of the dead man. Sindos, tomb 115. About 520 BC (case 22).

92. Bronze helmet and gold mask worn by the dead man. Sindos, tomb 115. About 520 BC (case 24).

93. Detail of an Attic kylix with an Amazonomachy scene. Sindos, tomb 115. About 520 BC (case 22).

ings is of special interest: in several tombs, containing both male and female burials, have been found miniature iron models of a waggon, a three-legged table, a chair, and spits with supports for roasting meat, all of which convey to us the despairing belief in a shadowy continuation after death of the daily needs of life (cases 17, 22, 26, 47 etc.).

Of the 36 tombs presented in the exhibition the most outstanding in terms of the wealth of jewellery found in them are the female tombs 20 (cases 11, 13-16) and 67 (cases 29-37, 39). Superb earrings in the filigree tech-

nique (cases 15, 33, 62), elaborate necklaces of braided silver and gold chain that end in snakes' heads (cases 16, 37), huge pins (cases 39, 53), distinctive jewellery made of coiled gold wire (cases 16, 33), pendants with granulated decoration (cases 15, 36 etc.), and gold masks (cases 27, 34 etc.), all dazzle us with their lavish use of gold. Men did not lag behind the women in decorating their clothes with large numbers of gold strips. The Archaic smile on the gold mask of the warrior in tomb 115 (case 24) radiates the same sense of mystery and sweetness as the kouroi contemporary with it, and his iron swords can be seen in identical form in Attic vase-painting.

Perfume from the East came to Chalastra in plastically modelled clay vases from Ionia (cases 25, 48) and in glass polychrome pots from Phoenicia (cases 1, 41, 46). The sea and travel were an integral part of the lives of the inhabitants of Chalastra. At that period, indeed, their city will have been on the coast, as is attested by the gold mouth-piece from tomb 28 (case 53), on which a boat with fish swimming around it is depicted in minute detail.

94. Gold mask worn by the dead woman. Sindos, tomb 56. About 510 BC (case 27).

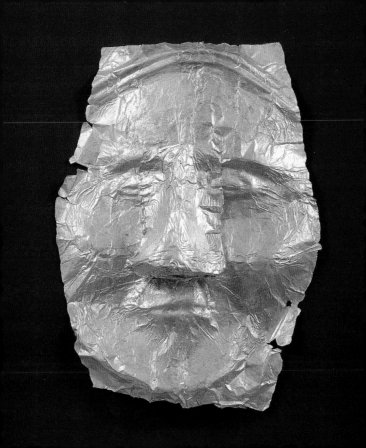

95. Item of jewellery made of coiled gold wire. Sindos, tomb 67. About 510 BC (case 33).

95

96. Gold jewellery.
Sindos, tomb 67. About
510 BC (case 37).

96

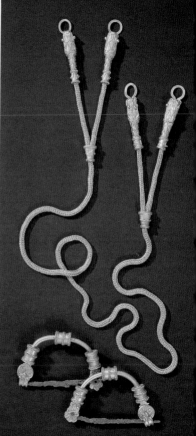

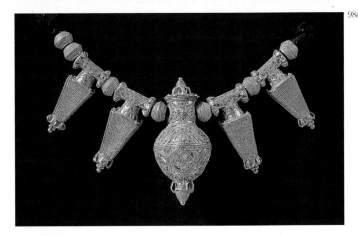

97-99 Elaborate gold jewellery that belonged to the dead woman in tomb 67
at Sindos. About 510 BC (cases 32, 35 and 36).

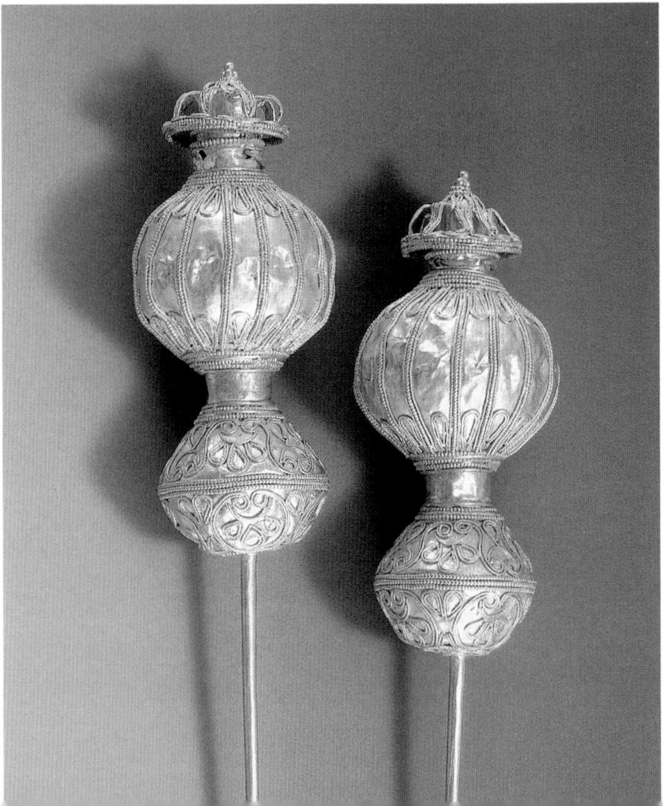

100. Superb gold pins. Sindos, tomb 67. About 510 BC (case 39).

*101. Silver bowl with a gold boss at the bottom. Sindos, tomb 52.
510-500 BC (case 45).*

102. *Detail of an Attic black-figure kylix with a Dionysiac scene. Sindos, tomb 52. 510-500 BC (case 45).*

103. *Attic black-figure krater, by the 'Louvre F6 painter'. Sindos, tomb 66. About 540 BC (case 44).*

102

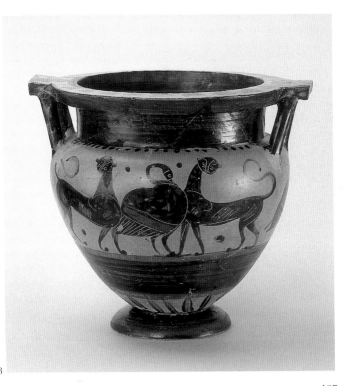

104. *Model of a waggon made of bronze sheet. Sindos, tomb 52.*
510-500 BC (case 47).

105. *Necklace made of elaborate gold beads. Sindos, tomb 28.*
About 560 BC (case 52).

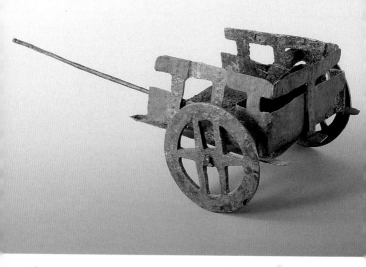

106

107

106. Gold piece depicting a ship. Sindos, tomb 28. About 560 BC (case 53).

107. Elaborate gold pins. Sindos, tomb 28. About 560 BC (case 53).

108. Gold earrings. Sindos, tomb 48. 525-500 BC (case 62).

VERGINA-DERVENI EXHIBITION

In 1977 and 1978 the lengthy investigations of Professor Manolis Andronikos at Vergina culminated in the exciting discovery of the unplundered tombs of Philip II and a young member of the royal family. An enormous mound (diam. 110 m.) covered these Macedonian tombs, each of which had two chambers and a façade in the Doric order. The bones of the two dead persons in the tomb of Philip were placed in gold caskets, and those in the tomb of the young member of the family in a silver hydria. They were surrounded by gold, silver, bronze and iron objects of unique quality which accompanied the deceased in their last resting place.

In the centre of the room (case 2) is displayed the gold casket of Philip II, who was murdered in the theatre at Aegae (modern Vergina) in 336 BC. It measures 41 x 34 x 20.5 cm. and is made of hammered gold sheet, weighing 7.820 mg. On its lid a rosette with inlays of blue glass paste is surrounded by sixteen relief rays, probably symbolizing the sun. This star-symbol is frequently found in Macedonia and probably had an official character, since it also adorned the shields of the soldiers. The sides of the coffer are adorned

109. Vergina. Model of the tomb of Philip II.

110. *Valuable, heavy gold wreath with oak leaves and acorns. From the tomb of Philip II. Third quarter of the 4th c. BC (case 2).*

111. *The gold casket that contained the bones of Philip II (case 2).*

with floral motifs of exceptional delicacy, and more rosettes with inlays of blue glass paste. Inside it were found the bones of the deceased, which had been washed after being cremated, and bore traces of the purple cloth in which they were wrapped. The relatively small size of the skeleton is striking; it is undoubtedly due in part to the fact that Philip was a short man, but is partly the result of the contraction of the bones as a result of the cremation. A heavy gold wreath of oak leaves and acorns was also found in the casket; evidence yielded by the excavation points to the conclusion that the dead king was wearing it when he was placed on the funeral pyre, but it was removed in time to prevent it melting completely under the high temperature of the fire.

The finds from the antechamber (cases 13-16) and main chamber (cases 2-12) of the tomb are on display around this central show case. The main, burial chamber yielded, amongst other things, the following unique objects:

An iron cuirass (case 3) decorated with gold strips, relief lions' heads, and a plaque on the side with the relief figure of the goddess Athena, patron goddess of warriors.

A gold and ivory shield and its bronze cover (case 4). The ivory

112. The iron cuirass of Philip II, decorated with gold strips (case 3).

112

117

emblem in the centre of the shield depicts a mythical hero vanquishing a woman. This is surrounded by circular zones in which the main decorative element is the meander pattern. The plaster that served as the background is covered by very fine gold leaf, and glass plaques are set in the spaces of the meander pattern. In the inner face of the shield relief figures of Victory decorate the ends of intersecting bands.

The iron weapons and bronze greaves of the dead king (case 5). The helmet was plain, made of iron and had a relief bust of Athena at the front; the larger of the two swords had gold decorative elements on the handle and ivory ones at the end of the scabbard. Another interesting

113. Iron 'Macedonian' helmet. From the tomb of Philip II (case 5).

114. Gold and ivory shield. From the tomb of Philip II (case 4).

114

115. Bronze tripod from the tomb of Philip II. 5th c. BC (case 9).

116. Large bronze cauldron on an iron tripod. From the tomb of Philip II (case 6).

115

and indeed unique find is the cylindrical bronze torch, blackened by the tow that it contained, which burned to light up the night.

Silver table-ware is displayed in two successive cases (7-8). The majority of the items are banquet vessels, oinochoe and situlae for the wine, ladles and a strainer to serve it, and drinking vessels in a variety of shapes: kylikes, kalykes and kantharoi. They are decorated with small relief heads of exceptional art, which are amongst the masterpieces of Greek metallurgy.

A bronze tripod (case 9) was a prize awarded at games held in honour of Hera at Argos, according to the inscription on the rim; it dates from the 5th c. BC and was probably a family heir-

loom belonging to the Macedonian royal house, which believed that it was descended from the Temenids of Argos.

The taste shown in the making of objects for every-day use is quite clear in the bronze lamp-holder (case 10), a pierced lantern which had a clay lamp fixed inside it.

One of the priceless finds from the tomb is the circular gilded silver diadem (case 12). It consists of two parts: the smaller tube covers the free ends of the

117. Silver amphoriskos. From the tomb of Philip II (case 7).

118-119. Silver banquet vessels. From the tomb of Philip II (cases 7 and 8).

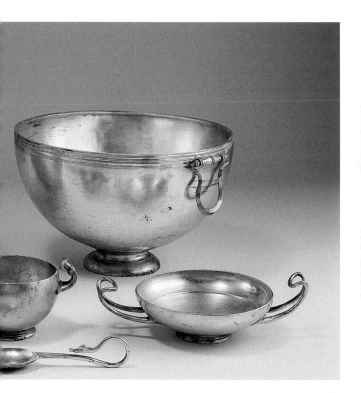

larger in such a way that the diameter of the diadem can be increased or decreased at will. Professor Andronikos believed that this was the diadem worn by the king in his capacity as high priest of his people.

In the antechamber of the tomb, as in the burial chamber, was found a stone chest containing a smaller, more simply decorated

120. Bronze lantern. From the tomb of Philip II (case 10).

121. Gilded silver diadem. From the tomb of Philip II (case 12).

gold casket, weighing 5.550 mg., though its contents were dazzling: a gold-embroidered cloth with a complex floral motif, of unique art and beauty (case 15), was used to wrap the bones of a young woman, to whom will have belonged the elegant, ethereal gold diadem, with flowers and palmettes blown in the wind at the ends of gold stalks, and tiny bees buzzing around them (case 16). The antechamber also contained other valuable finds. A wreath with small branches and myrtle flowers (case 13) and three objects of military nature (case 14), which were leaning against the marble door leading to the main burial chamber and were probably offerings to the dead king,

21

122. Part of an ivory plaque from the decoration of a wooden couch, depicting Dionysos and a Silenus crowned with ivy. From the tomb of Philip II (case 12).

122

123. Ivory heads from the decoration of a wooden couch. The two at the top are possibly portraits of Philip and Alexander. From the tomb of Philip II (case 12).

whose interment was conducted in great haste: a pair of gilded bronze greaves, an iron pectoral covered with a gilded sheet of silver worked in relief, and a gold quiver-case (gorytos) with relief scenes of the fall of Troy. These last two objects, which are

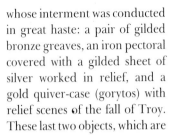

124

124.
Gold gorgoneion from a small box. From the tomb of Philip II (case 13).

125.
Gold wreath with myrtle leaves and flowers. From the tomb of Philip II (case 13).

125

126. *Gilded iron pectoral, probably the spoils of wars.*
From the tomb of Philip II (case 14).

127. *Gilded silver gorytos (quiver-case). From the tomb of Philip II (case 14).*

126

foreign to the Greek panoply, were probably spoils taken by Philip during his wars against the Thracians and Scythians.

The tomb of the young member of the royal family (the so-called 'Tomb of the Prince') also contained a complete set of silver vessels (cases 17, 20), and a unique sight was provided by the silver cinerary hydria (case 19), which was found in the tomb with a large gold wreath of oak leaves and acorns placed around its neck. Another rare find is the silver-plated iron lamp-holder, on which a terracotta lamp was placed (case 21). Parts of the ivory decoration of the wooden couch that was placed in the burial chamber of the tombs – as in the case of the tomb of Philip – have survived

128. *Piece of gold-embroidered purple cloth, in which the bones of the dead woman found in the antechamber of the tomb of Philip II were wrapped (case 15).*

129. *The gold casket that contained the bones of the dead woman in the antechamber of the tomb of Philip II (case 16).*

(case 19): these are certainly the finest examples of ivory-carving of the 4th c. BC, especially the three-figure Dionysiac group, showing a drunken Silenus supported on the shoulders of a young Maenad, preceded by goat-footed Pan, playing his pipes.

The importance of the discoveries at Vergina for the history of Ancient Macedonia became even clearer after the publication of the inscriptions from the 47 grave stelai discovered in the earth deposits of the Great Tumulus. They have yielded valuable new linguistic material, mostly names, of undoubtedly Greek origins, covering the period from

130. Elegant female diadem from the antechamber of the tomb of Philip II (case 16).

the late 5th to the early 3rd c. BC. A gold medallion dating from the 3rd c. AD has a bust that is thought to be a portrait of Olympias, the mother of Alexander the Great (case 26).

The rest of this room is devoted to finds from tombs contemporary with those at Vergina, from the area around Thessalonike: Stavroupolis (cases 22, 24-25) and Sedes (case 23) produced some fine gold jewellery and metal vases, while the tumuli at Nea Michaniona (ancient Aeneia) concealed tombs that, while poorer

131. Frying-pan vessel. From the 'tomb of the prince' at Vergina (case 20).

132. Silver cinerary hydria and the gold oak wreath around its neck. From the 'tomb of the prince' at Vergina (case 19).

*133. Ivory plaque with a depiction of the god Sabazios.
From the 'tomb of the prince' at Vergina (case 19).*

*134. Ivory plaque depicting a drunken Silenus and Maenad accompanied by Pan.
From the 'tomb of the prince' at Vergina (case 19).*

in terms of the offerings they contained (cases 27-28), were finely painted with palmette motifs, and depictions of objects hanging from nails or resting on shelves, including a snow-white dove. Gold and silver objects dating from the 4th c. BC were also found in tombs at Potidaia (case 29).

The main group in this part of the room comes from the tombs discovered at Derveni near Thessalonike (cases 30-41). Though they were much smaller than the Vergina tombs, with which they were contemporary, dating from the middle of the second half of the 4th c. BC, they contained dozens of precious vases made of bronze and silver, gold wreaths, and superb necklaces, all of them witnesses to the astonishing flowering of metallurgy in Macedonia in the 4th c. BC. The finest find of all is the famous bronze krater (0.91 m. high), a unique masterpiece with no known parallels (case 30). It is made by two techniques – the rim, handles, base and the statuettes on the shoulders are cast, and the relief figures on the body and neck are cast and hammered. The mouth is covered by a perforated concave lid, which acted as a strainer for the wine.

The decorative scheme is taken from the Dionysiac cycle, which was of course consistent with the

135. Marble grave stele of Harpalos. From Vergina. About 350- 325 BC.

136. Marble grave stele of a hoplite. From Vergina. 430-420 BC.

136

137. Bronze vessels from a tomb at Stavroupolis near Thessalonike. Late 5th c. BC (case 22).

138. Pyxis with 'West Slope' decoration, and a black-glazed skyphos. From a tomb at Sedes near Thessalonike. Last quarter of the 4th c. BC (case 23).

original purpose of the vessel, to contain wine, the gift of Dionysos to mankind. The relief composition on the body of the vase is dominated by the sacred couple of Dionysos and Ariadne, serene, blessed and eternally young, in striking contrast with the orgiastic atmosphere of the ecstatic

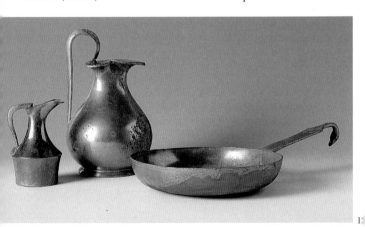

bacchic dance of the Maenads and Satyrs surrounding them. The bearded man wearing a single sandal is an intrusive figure, and has provoked much debate: he is possibly the Thracian king Lykourgos, who met a tragic death after his profane penetration of the mysteries of the Maenads, or the 'weak' hunter Pentheus, who met with the same fate as Lykourgos. The four seated figures on the shoulders of the krater, the young Dionysos, and the Silenus and Maenads wearied by the dance, are amongst the masterpieces of ancient Greek bronze sculpture.

145

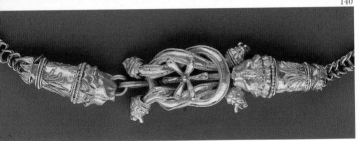

139. *Gold ornament from a tomb at Stavroupolis near Thessalonike. Late 4th c. BC (case 24).*

140. *Gold necklace. From a tomb at Sedes near Thessalonike. Last quarter of the 4th c. BC (case 23).*

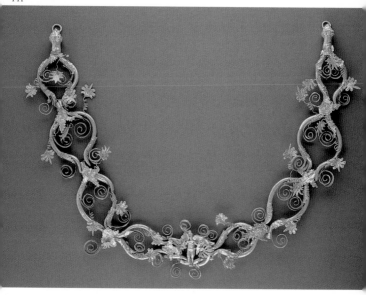

141. *Elaborate gold ornament (a wreath or diadem), with a naked Eros in the centre on leaves. From a tomb at Stavroupolis near Thessalonike. Late 4th c. BC (case 23).*

The inlaid letters on the rim of the krater spell out the name in the Thessalian dialect of the owner of the krater, who was from Larisa: Asteiounios, son of Anaxagoras from Larisa. The presence of the krater in a tomb in Macedonia is probably to be accounted for by a historical event: in 344 BC, Philip took to Macedonia hostages from the aristocratic clan of the Aleuadai of Larisa, who had taken part in an independence movement.

The papyrus from tomb A (case 41), which contains a philosophical, Orphic text, is the earliest surviving papyrus with a Greek text (350-325 BC).

142. Gold myrtle wreath from a tomb at Stavroupolis near Thessalonike. Late 4th c. BC (case 24).

149

143. *Folding bronze pen and ink case. From a tomb at Stavroupolis near Thessalonike. Late 4th c. BC (case 24).*

144. *Silver stool (diphros) from a tomb at Stavroupolis near Thessalonike. Late 4th c. BC (case 25).*

1

145. *Gold medallion for games held at Beroia in honour of Alexander the Great. AD 225-250 (case 26).*

146. *Jewellery and a plate from a tomb in a tumulus at Nea Michaniona (ancient Aeneia). 350-325 BC (case 28).*

146

147-148. Details from the painted decoration of tomb II from tumulus A at Nea Michaniona (ancient Aeneia). 350-325 BC.

149-152. The famous bronze krater of Derveni. It has cast and hammered decoration of superb art, with subjects drawn from the Dionysiac cycle. It was found in tomb B and had been used as an ossuary. 330-310 BC (case 30).

150

1

153-154. Bronze banquet vessels.
From tomb B at Derveni.
330-310 BC (cases 31 and 33).

155. Silver vases. From tomb B at Derveni. 330-310 BC (case 32).

156. Silver strainer. From tomb B at Derveni. 330-310 BC (case 31).

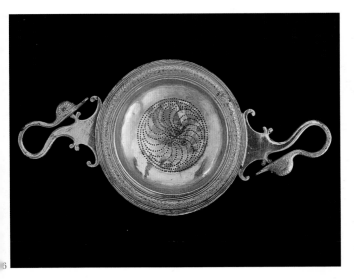

157. *Small silver oinochoe with gilded floral decoration. From tomb B at Derveni. 330-310 BC (case 32).*

158. *Detail from the interior of a silver kalyx. From tomb Z at Derveni. 330-310 BC (case 39).*

159. *Deep silver plate with tongue-pattern decoration. From tomb B at Derveni. 330-310 BC (case 32).*

157

9

160. *Drinking cup of translucent glass. From tomb B at Derveni.*
330-310 BC (case 32).

161. *Gold myrtle wreath. From tomb B at Derveni.*
330-310 BC (case 32).

167

162-163. Bronze situla decorated with a bust of a Silenus at the lower handle attachment. From tomb A at Derveni. 330-310 BC (case 35).

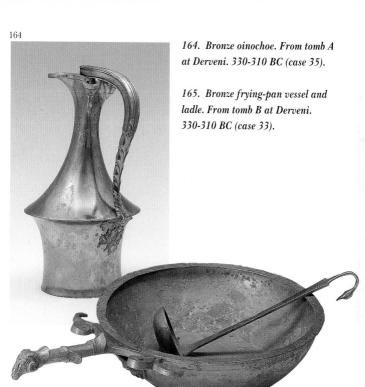

164

164. Bronze oinochoe. From tomb A at Derveni. 330-310 BC (case 35).

165. Bronze frying-pan vessel and ladle. From tomb B at Derveni. 330-310 BC (case 33).

165

166. Bronze greaves. From tomb B at Derveni. 330-310 BC (case 31).

167. Bronze lantern. From tomb A at Derveni. 330-310 BC (case 36).

168. Bronze volute krater; it had been used as a cinerary urn. From tomb A at Derveni. 330-310 BC (case 37).

166

168

169. *Elaborate gold earring.*
From tomb Z at Derveni. 330-310 BC
(case 39).

170. *Gold finger-ring. From tomb Z*
at Derveni. 330-310 BC (case 39).

171. *Gold myrtle wreath. From tomb*
D at Derveni. 330-310 BC (case 38).

170

172. *Gold jewellery and a terracotta pyxis. From tomb Z at Derveni. 330-310 BC (case 39).*

173. *Pair of gold earrings. From the area of ancient Lete. Late 4th c. BC (case 42).*

*174. Pair of elaborate gold earrings with vase-shaped attachments.
From the area of Lete. Late 4th c. BC (case 42).*

*175-176. Gold necklace and finger-ring. From tomb Z at Derveni.
330-310 BC (case 39).*

ARCHAIC AND EARLY CLASSICAL PERIODS

Temporary Exhibition

The coasts of Chalkidike and Pieria were settled by several waves of migrants-colonists in the late 8th and 7th c. BC, the period of the great movements of Greek populations known as the second Greek colonization; several settlements, however, perhaps go back to the first colonization at the end of the 2nd millennium BC. The colonists came mainly from Eretria and Chalkis, though also from Andros and Corinth.

Intensive trade with Ionia, Aeolis, Corinth, Euboea and Attica in the 7th and 6th centuries, together with the exploitation of the timber and rich mines of Chalkidike, brought great economic prosperity, which is reflected in the finds from the 7th, 6th and 5th c. BC cemeteries at Sindos, Therme and Ayia Paraskevi.

Excavation evidence suggests that there was a sanctuary of Artemis at Sani. Terracotta figurines, and Corinthian, Ionian, Chian and Attic vases have been found here by which the acme of the sanctuary has been dated from the late 7th to the middle of the 5th c. BC.

At Mende, an Eretrian colony, parts of the city and cemetery have been excavated. As at other

177. Multi-coloured Chian kalyx. From a tomb at Ayia Paraskevi in Thessalonike. 6th c. BC (case 3).

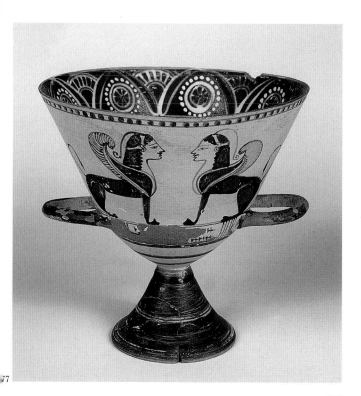

178. *Detail from an Attic black-figure vase. From a tomb at Ayia Paraskevi in Thessalonike. 525-500 BC (case 4).*

179. *Bronze hydria. From the cemetery at Pydna in Pieria. Late 6th c. BC (case 8).*

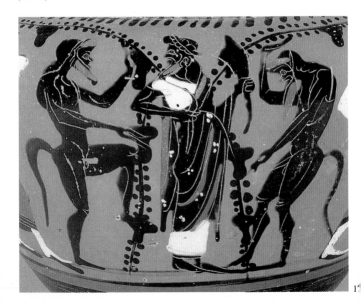

cities in Chalkidiki, the bodies – mainly of infants and children – were placed in pithoi. The funerary vases from the cemetery at Polychronos reveal the use of traditional motifs alongside floral decoration imported directly from Aeolis in Asia Minor.

The enormous cemetery of ancient Akanthos, an Andriote colony on the coast near Ierissos, dates from the 6th c. BC down to Roman times. Amongst the countless grave offerings, some outstanding examples of Attic black- and red-figure pottery are a distinctive presence.

The majority of the tombs in the cemetery at Ai-Yannis Nikitis, along with the offerings found in them, belong to the 7th c. BC, and are restricted to local prehistoric pottery.

At Torone, the powerful colony of Chalkis, excavations have uncovered parts of the city, and also an important Protogeometric cemetery.

The 5th c. BC tombs uncovered at Pydna in Pieria attest to the

180. White Attic lekythos. From the cemetery at Pydna in Pieria. Second half of the 5th c. BC (case 8).

181-182. Both sides of a two-sided kantharos. From the cemetery at ancient Akanthos. 480-470 BC (case 22).

wealth of the occupants of the city: gold and silver jewellery has been found, along with choice Attic vases, and bronze vases pointing to relations with the Greek colonies of South Italy.

The flowering of the coastal cities continued until the middle of the 4th c. BC. The destruction of Olynthos (348 BC) and the domination of Philip II meant the transfer of the economic centres to the cities founded and supported by the Macedonian kings.

183. Clay vase from a local workshop (detail). From Pyrgadikia in Chalkidike. Middle of the 5th c. BC (pedestal 25).

PREHISTORIC COLLECTION

ROOM 11

Temporary Exhibition

Important excavations of the last decade in prehistoric tumuli (earth mounds formed by the accumulated debris of the ruins of successive brick-built houses) at Kastanas, Assiros and Toumba in Thessalonike have awakened interest in the investigation of prehistoric Macedonia.

Room 11 houses characteristic finds of the Late Bronze Age and Early Iron Age from Assiros and Kastanas. Local imitations of Mycenaean vases attest to the penetration of the Mycenaean civilization. The discovery at Assiros of large numbers of storage rooms in which large quantities of grain could be gathered has furnished evidence for the study of the social organization of the community.

The rest of the room is devoted to finds from Central and West Macedonia, presented in chronological order. The Middle Neolithic period (4400-3200 BC) is represented by vases from Servia near Kozani and by sherds from the Neolithic settlement III at Vasilika. In the Late Neolithic period (3200-2500 BC) the above sites were joined by the settlement on the south hill at Olynthos, from which we have several stone and terracotta figurines.

184. Hoard of bronze axes from Petralona in Chalkidike (case 8).

185. Clay cups. From Mesimeri near Thessalonike. Early Bronze Age (case 8).

186. Clay kantharoi. From Armenochori near Florina. Early Bronze Age (case 8).

The Early Bronze Age (2500-2000 BC) is represented by a large number of finds from Mesimeri near Thessalonike, Axiochori and Kalindria in Central Macedonia, and Armenochori near Florina.

18.

From the Middle Bronze Age (2000-1600 BC) comes the wheel-made grey 'Minyan' pottery from Ayios Mamas and Molyvo-pyrgos in Chalkidike, which was created in the coastal regions.

The hoard of bronze axes from Petralona in Chalkidike is of particular interest for the study of early metal-working.

In the Late Bronze Age (1600-1100 BC) the production continued of monochrome burnished ware and incised with applied

paint ware, while at the same time matt-painted ware made its appearance with the importing of Mycenaean pottery. Typical examples of the latter were found at Kalindria and the recent excavations at Assiros and Kastanas.

The categories of pottery found in the Bronze Age continued into the Early Iron Age (1100-700 BC). West Macedonia played an important role in the production of matt-painted pottery, while the coasts were exposed to influences from the Geometric style of the South. The tumulus cemetery at Vergina is a meeting ground for old and new cultural currents, while bronze jewellery and iron weaponry are found in abundance in tombs throughout the whole of Macedonia.

'Macedonian bronzes' – cast pendants in a variety of shapes – make their appearance at the end of this period. The simple decorative motifs of the Early Iron Age, and the monochrome burnished and grey pottery were to survive until the end of the Archaic period, which coincided with the end of the Persian Wars.

187. *Jug from the tumulus at Assiros. Early Iron Age (case 7).*

188. *Vase from Ayios Mamas in Chalkidike. Early Bronze Age (case 9).*

189. *Bronze jewellery from Axiochori in Kilkis and the tumulus cemetery at Vergina. Early Iron Age (cases 16 and 17).*

TRANSLATION: Dr. DAVID HARDY

DESIGN: RACHEL MISDRACHI-KAPON

ARTISTIC ADVISOR: MOSES KAPON

DESKTOP PUBLISHING: PANOS STAMATAS

COLOUR SEPARATIONS: GRAFFITI S.A.

PRINTING: EPIKINONIA LTD

BINDING: D. TSIAMALOS

191